BUILDING BLOCKS OF PHYSICAL SCIENCE

MATTER AND HOW IT CHANGES

Written by Joseph Midthun

Illustrated by Samuel Hiti

a Scott Fetzer company
Chicago

World Book, Inc.
180 North LaSalle Street
Suite 900
Chicago, Illinois 60601
USA

For information about other World Book publications, visit our website at **www.worldbook.com** or call **1-800-WORLDBK (967-5325).**
For information about sales to schools and libraries, call 1-800-975-3250 (United States), or 1-800-837-5365 (Canada).

Library of Congress Cataloging-in-Publication Data for this volume has been applied for.

Building Blocks of Physical Science
ISBN: 978-0-7166-4460-6 (set, hc.)

Matter and How It Changes
ISBN: 978-0-7166-4468-2 (hc.)

Also available as:
ISBN: 978-0-7166-4478-1 (e-book)

Acknowledgments:
Created by Samuel Hiti and Joseph Midthun
Art by Samuel Hiti
Additional art by David Shephard/The Bright Agency
Additional spot art by Dreamstime and Shutterstock
Text by Joseph Midthun

TABLE OF CONTENTS

There is a glossary on page 39. Terms defined in the glossary are in type **that looks like this** on their first appearance.

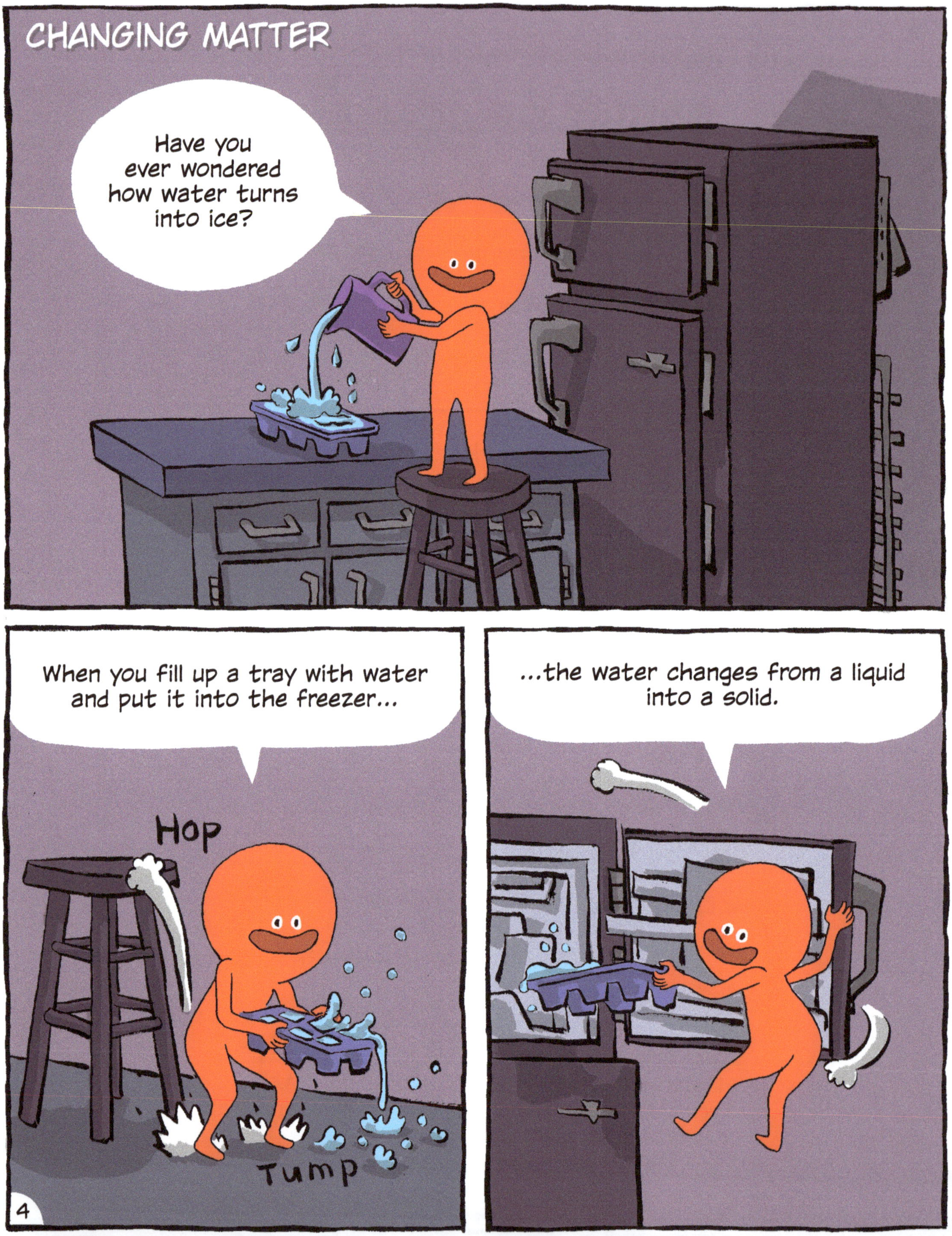

Have you ever wondered how water turns into ice?

This is just one of many ways that matter can change.

But what, you may ask, is matter?

Oh...
Where are my manners?
Scrush...

ZIP

I'm **MATTER.**
Everything in the world is made of me!
SHUSH

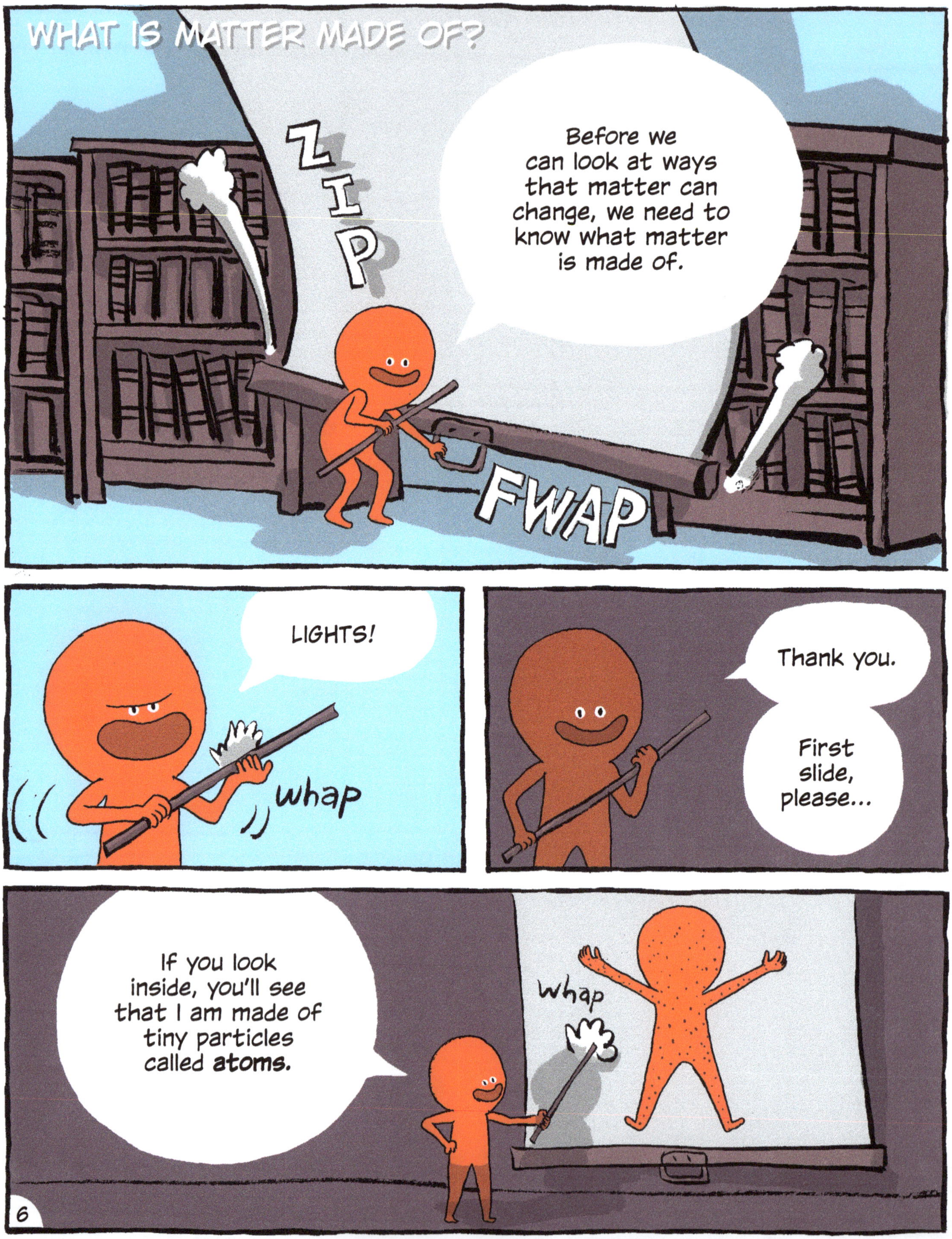

WHAT IS MATTER MADE OF?

ZIP

Before we can look at ways that matter can change, we need to know what matter is made of.

FWAP

Atoms are the basic units of matter.
whap

When atoms bond together, they form **molecules.**

LIGHTS, PLEASE!
Let's take a closer look at ice.

It's made of molecules of two hydrogen atoms and one oxygen atom, just like liquid water.

So how come it's frozen solid and not a liquid?
snap

Simple!
Matter can change states, or forms.

There are three basic **states of matter:** solids, liquids, and gases.

The molecules in a SOLID vibrate. They are arranged in a repeating pattern, like soldiers marching together.

The molecules in a LIQUID move more freely, like people walking in a large group.

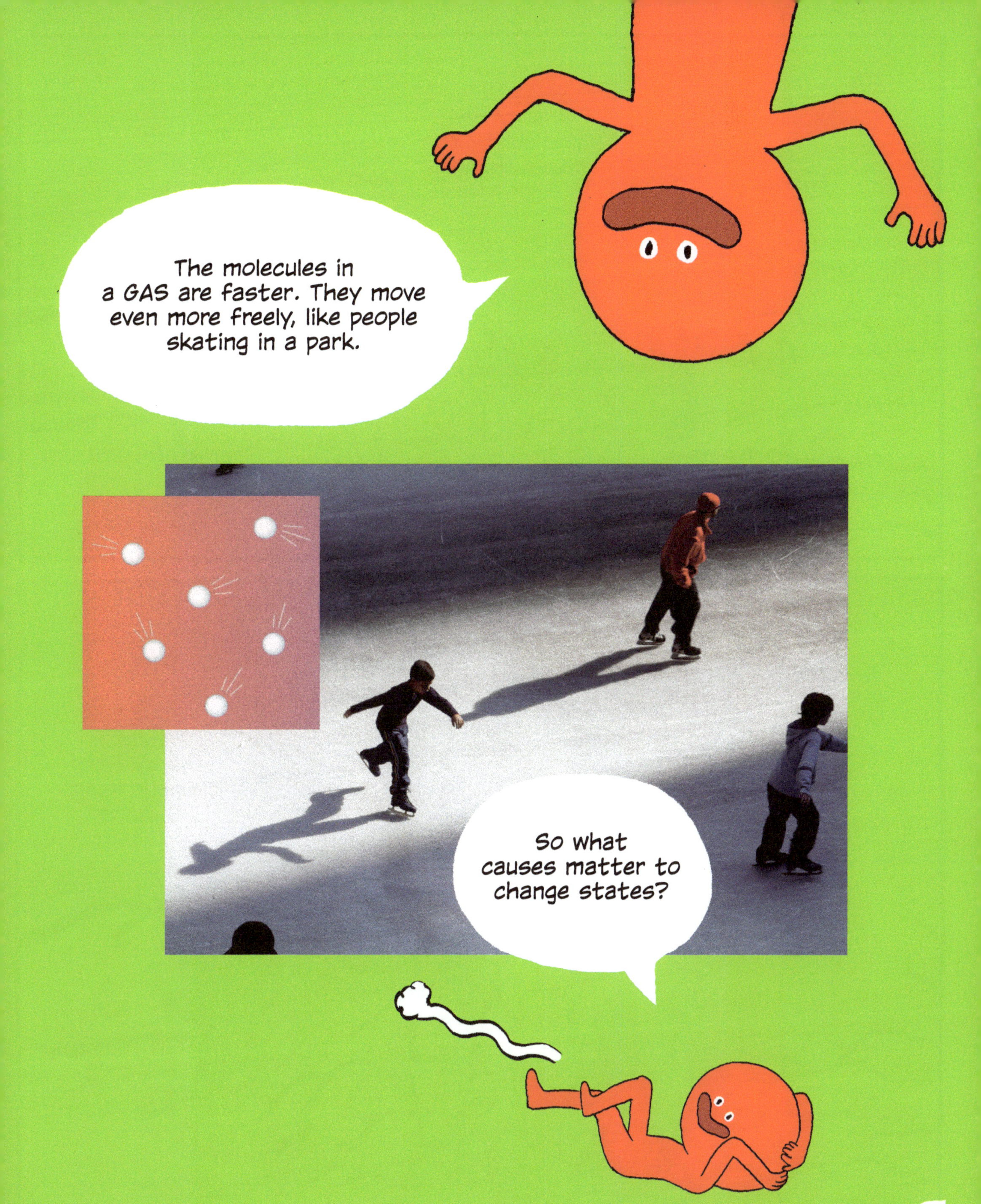

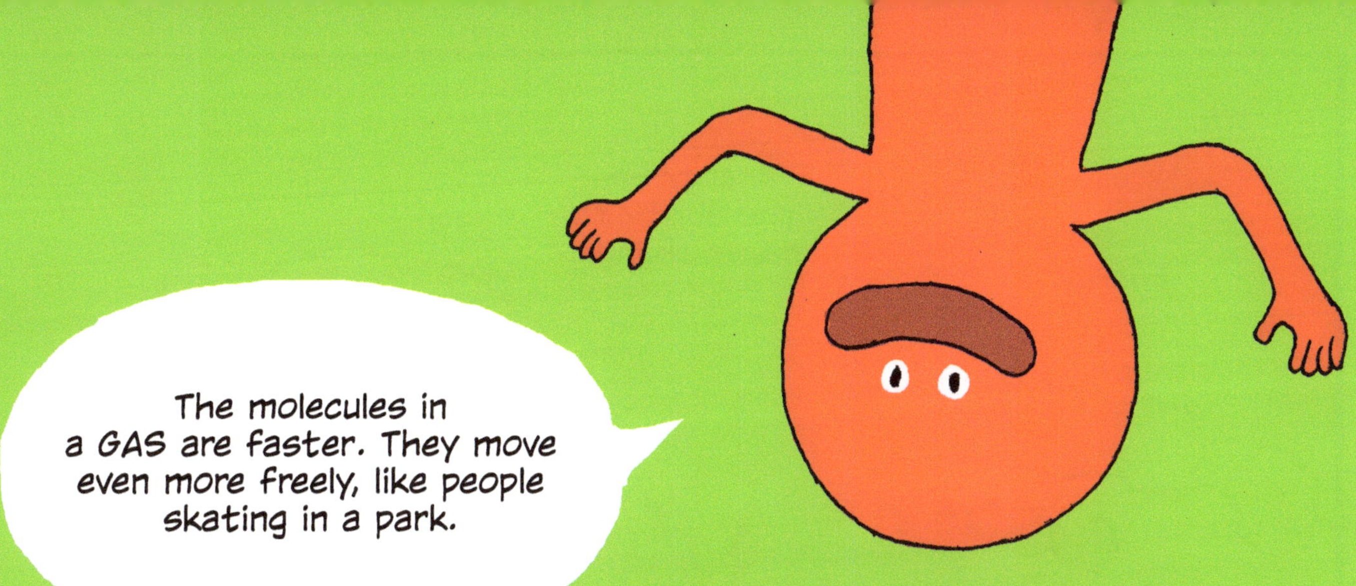

So what causes matter to change states?

HEATING MATTER

Energy!

Energy has the ability to cause change.

Heat is a form of energy.

Heat energy from the sun keeps us warm.

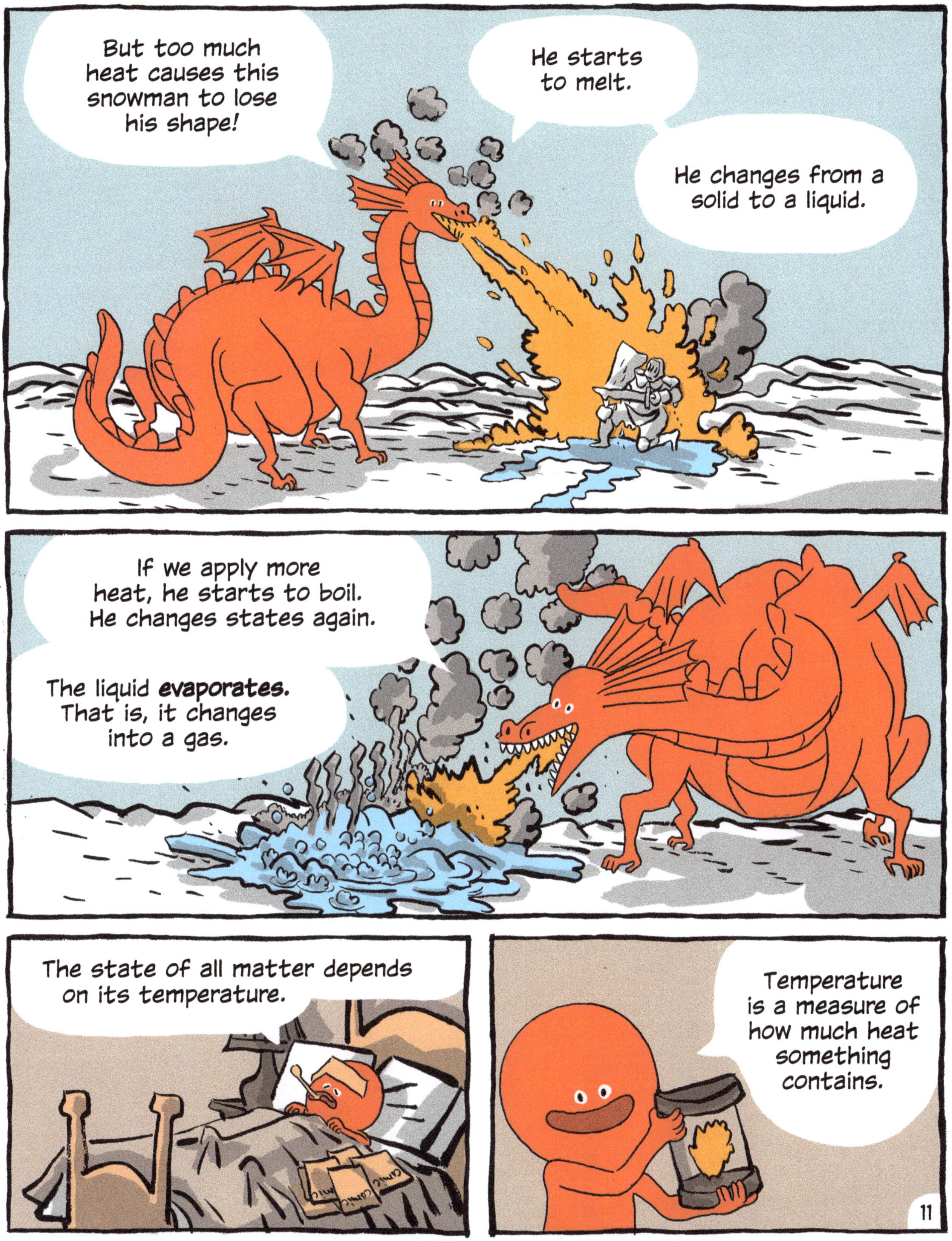

But too much heat causes this snowman to lose his shape!

He starts to melt.

He changes from a solid to a liquid.

So far, we've changed a solid to a liquid to a gas.

But matter can also change in the reverse direction—from a gas to a liquid to a solid.

Try this.

Make sure your hand is clean and dry.

Now put your hand in front of your mouth and breathe on it.

Your hand will feel damp. Why? The answer is **condensation.**

Your breath contains **water vapor,** a gas. When a gas is cooled, the molecules condense, or bundle together.

The gas changes into a liquid.

Your hand is cooler than the inside of your body, so the water vapor changes into liquid water when it hits your hand.

We can see condensation when we breathe on a window. As the water vapor from your breath cools down, tiny droplets of liquid water collect on the glass.

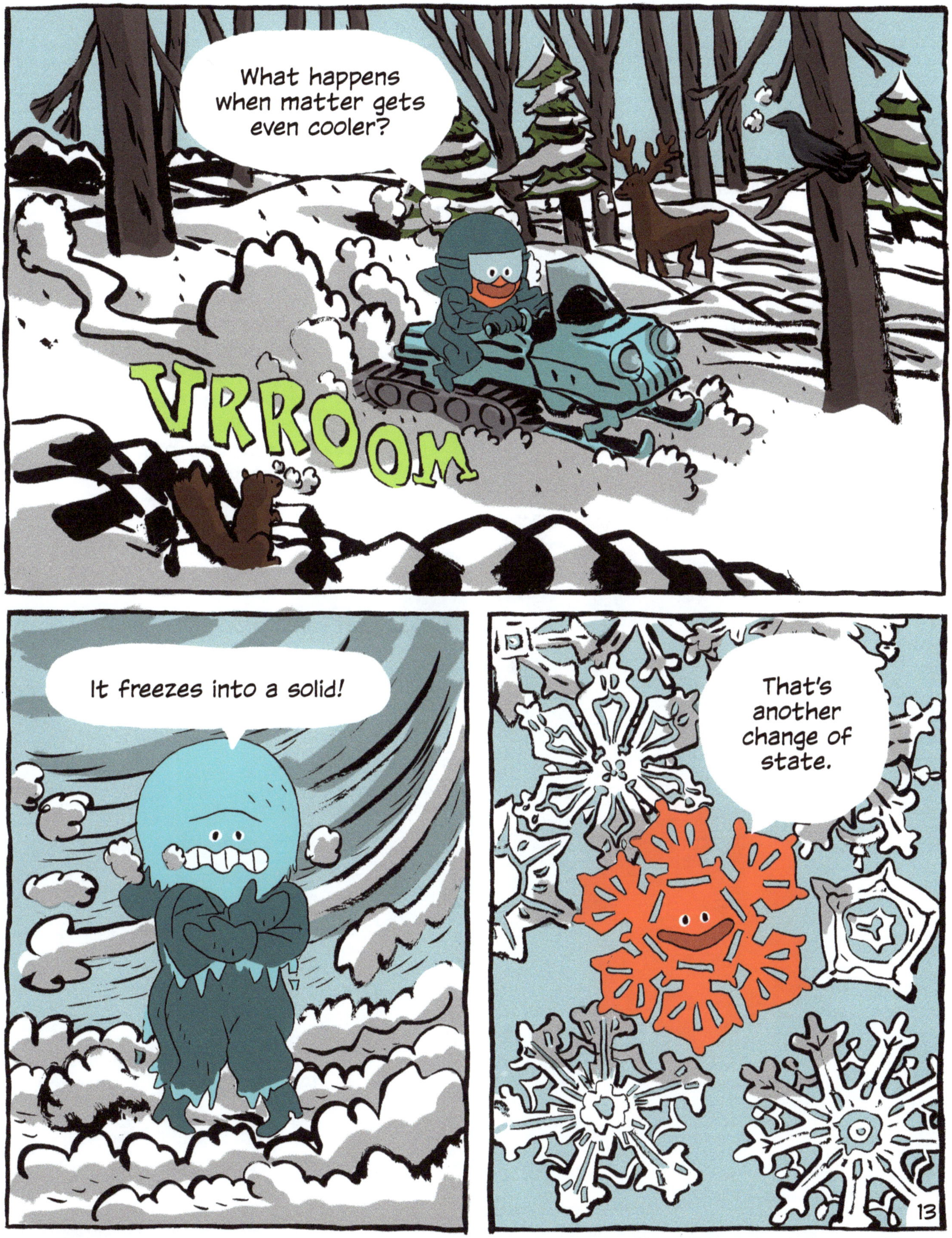

What happens when matter gets even cooler?

VRROOM

...AND BACK AND FORTH

The tiny droplets stick together and form larger droplets. These droplets fall back to Earth as rain.
If it is cold enough outside, rain can freeze as it falls, changing from a liquid into a solid—snow!
scoop

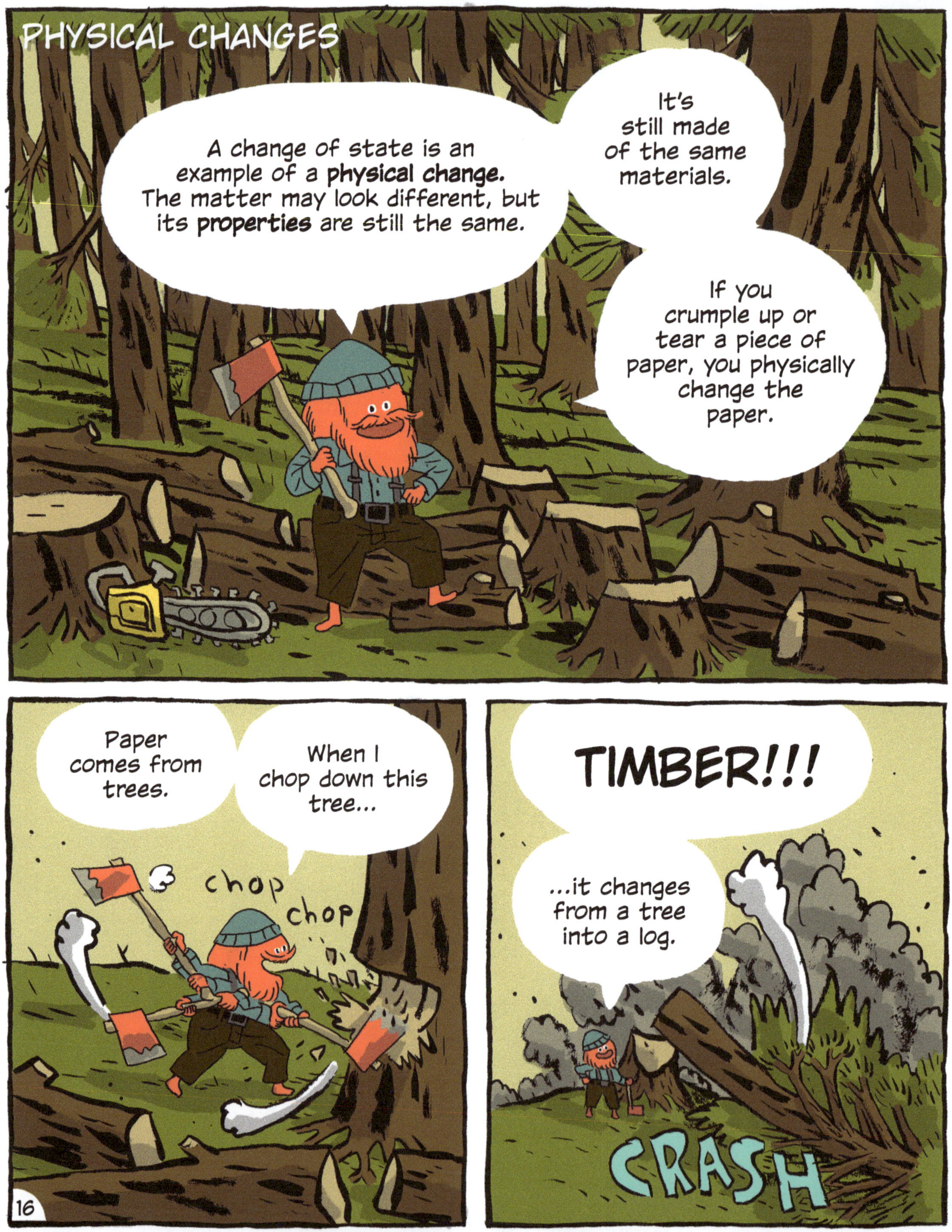

PHYSICAL CHANGES

A change of state is an example of a **physical change.** The matter may look different, but its **properties** are still the same.

It's still made of the same materials.

If you crumple up or tear a piece of paper, you physically change the paper.

I can carve this log with a chain saw.

VVVRRR
ZIP

Now all that's left is some sawdust...
BUZ

...and a toothpick!
The tree has just undergone a few physical changes, but it is still wood.

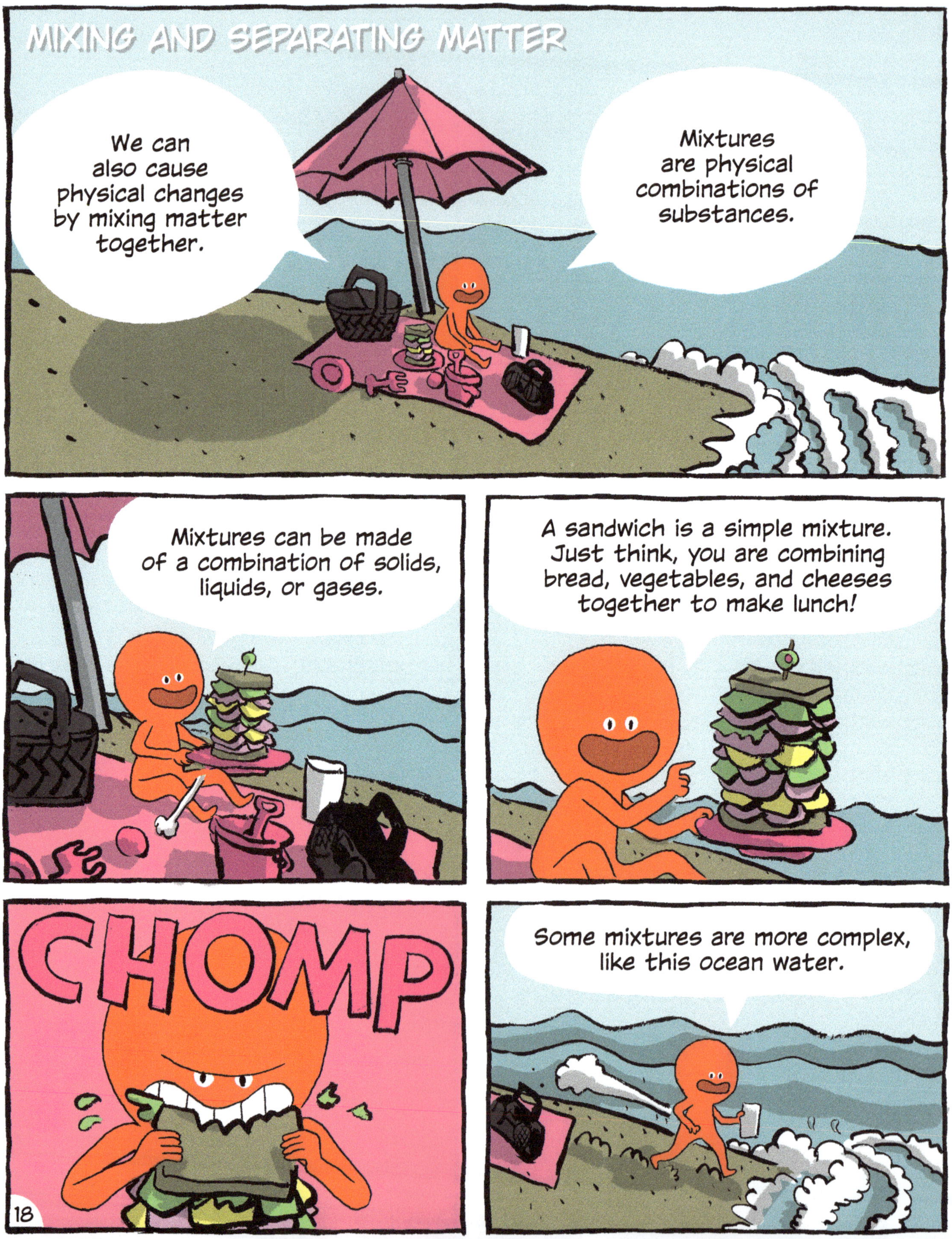

MIXING AND SEPARATING MATTER

We can also cause physical changes by mixing matter together.

Mixtures are physical combinations of substances.

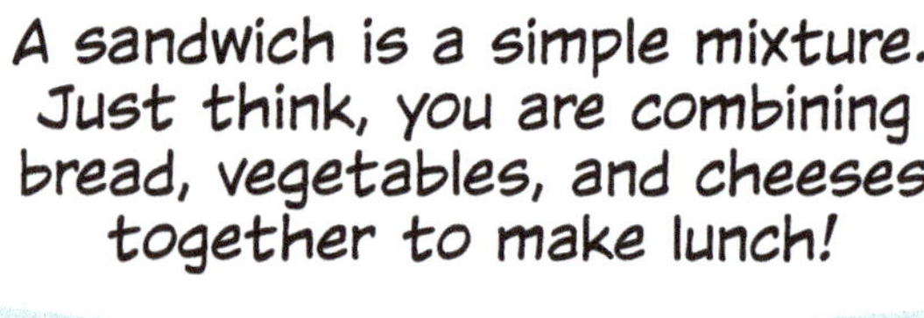

The movement of the ocean keeps water and sand evenly mixed.
SCOOP

But if the water is kept still, the larger pieces of sand will settle to the bottom.

This kind of mixture is called a **suspension.**

A suspension is kept mixed by the movement of one or both substances.

When the substances separate, they are no longer a suspension.

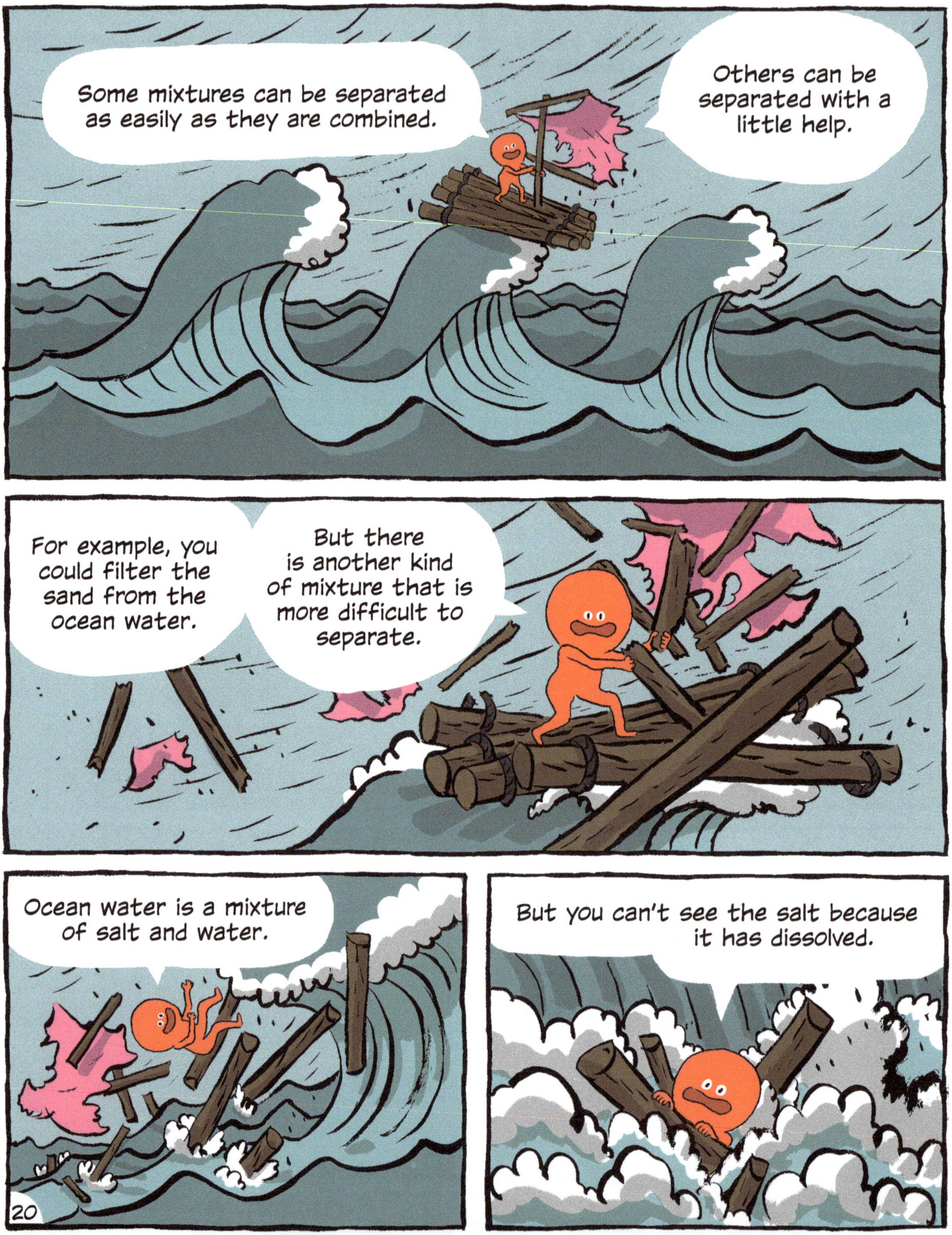

Some mixtures can be separated as easily as they are combined.

Others can be separated with a little help.

That means it is mixed evenly into the water.

This kind of mixture is called a **solution.**

No matter how still you keep ocean water, the salt will never settle to the bottom.

To separate the salt from the water, we need to wait for the sun to evaporate the water.

The solution has been separated!
The salt is left behind.
Agua...

CHEMICAL CHANGES

So far we've talked about physical changes to matter.

When I carved the sculpture, I didn't change the basic properties of wood.

But what happens when I toss wood into a fire?

whoop

Fire causes the wood to burn. This is a **chemical change.**

A chemical change causes different kinds of matter to form.

Smoke and ash are made from the carbon, hydrogen, and oxygen atoms that were in the tree.

This piece of iron has rust on it.

CLank

Rusting happens when iron combines with oxygen to make an orange color.

Chemical changes are more common than you might think. Here are some other examples of chemical changes:

When humans eat food, their bodies break down the food into basic **nutrients** that are used for energy.

Green plants use the energy from the sun to combine carbon dioxide and water to make "food" and store it.

Plants use the food energy to live and grow.

PHOTOSYNTHESIS

Humans and other animals can then **absorb** that energy by eating plants or by eating animals that eat plants. They can also release the energy by burning the plant.

COOKING

Food spoils when the tiny living things called **microbes** multiply on the food and begin to eat it.

Microbes produce gases and other chemicals, causing changes in flavor or odor. Rotten food smells bad because of the gases given off by microbes.

FOOD SPOILAGE

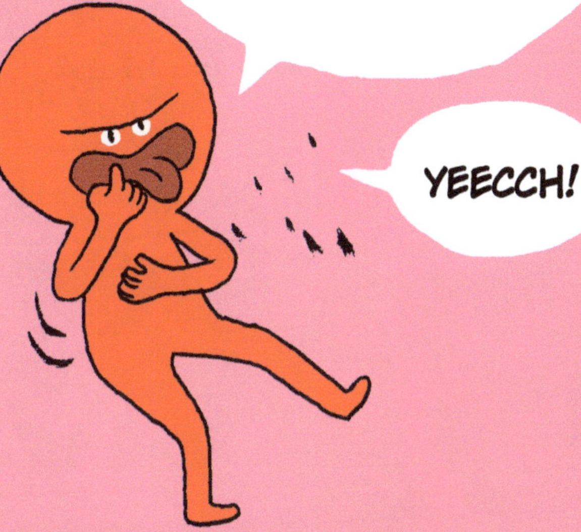

CHANGES AROUND US
Matter changes around us all the time.

Can you think about where you have seen matter change in your day-to-day life?

How about steam coming from radiators...

Or even smoke from a chimney?

tie
tie
tie

Or what about food?

Have you ever seen someone bake bread? What happens when you put the dough in the oven?

SUPER STATES

Scientists study matter and its different states in laboratories around the world.

They have even discovered some other states of matter!

Super-cold substances create an unusual state of matter.

Superfluids are created by cooling atoms to extremely low temperatures.

A superfluid is a liquid that can behave like a gas.

Liquid

Gas

Helium in a superfluid state can creep up the side of its container and crawl over the lip!

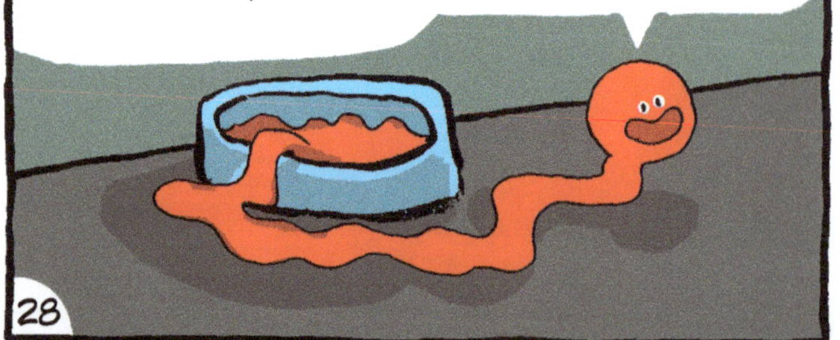

Helium is lighter than air. It is the only **element** that never turns into a solid.

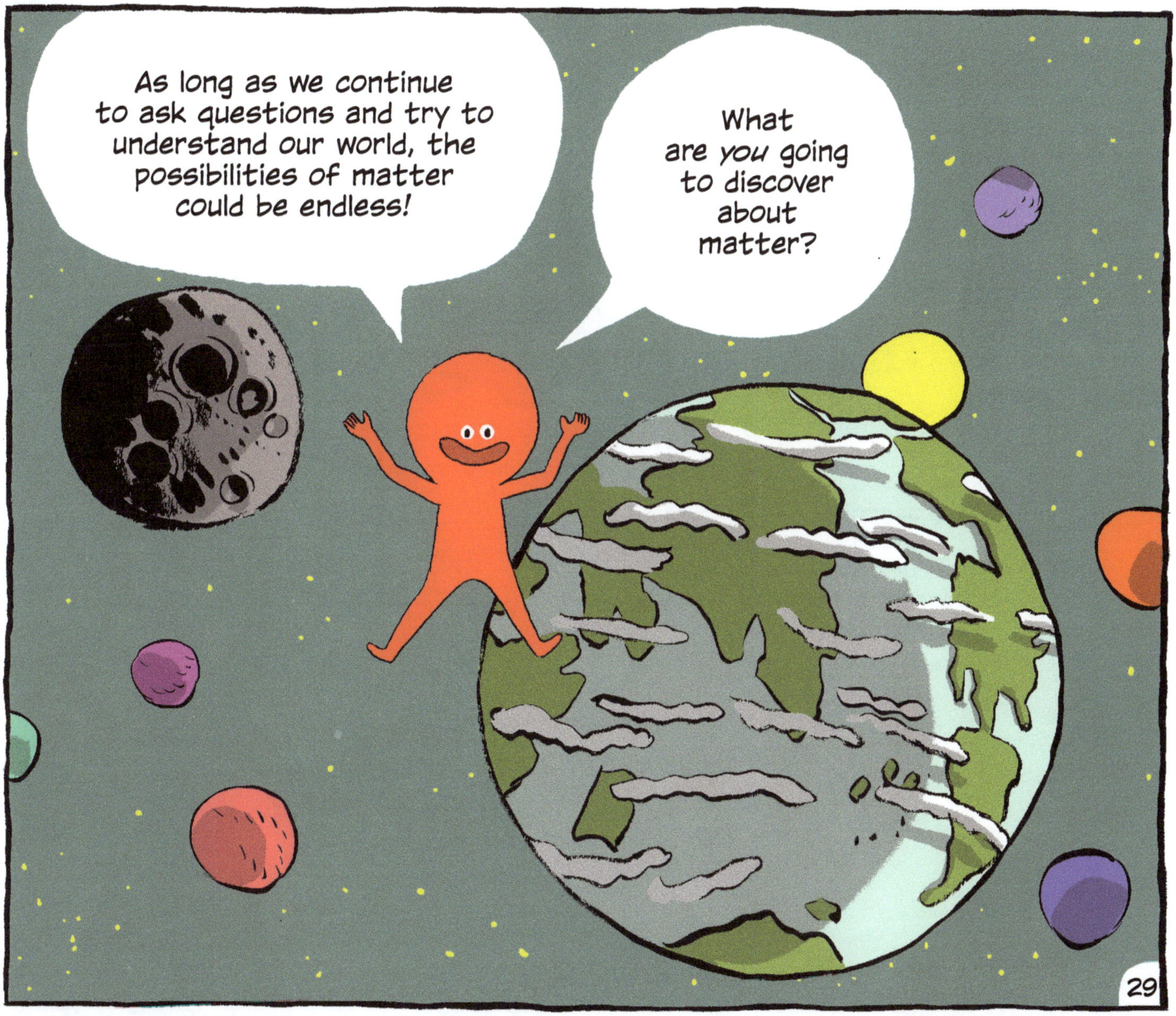

As long as we continue to ask questions and try to understand our world, the possibilities of matter could be endless!

What are *you* going to discover about matter?

TIMELINE

429 B.C.

Greek philosopher Empedocles argued that all matter was composed of four elements: fire, air, water, and earth.

79

Roman philosopher Pliny described *ferrum corrumpitur* (spoiled iron) that we call rust.

1867

Swedish chemist Alfred Nobel patented dynamite, a powerful explosive that can be handled safely.

1896

French physicist Henri Becquerel discovered radioactivity while studying uranium.

1898

Polish scientist Marie Skłodowska Curie coined the term "radioactivity" to describe the activity of certain kinds of matter.

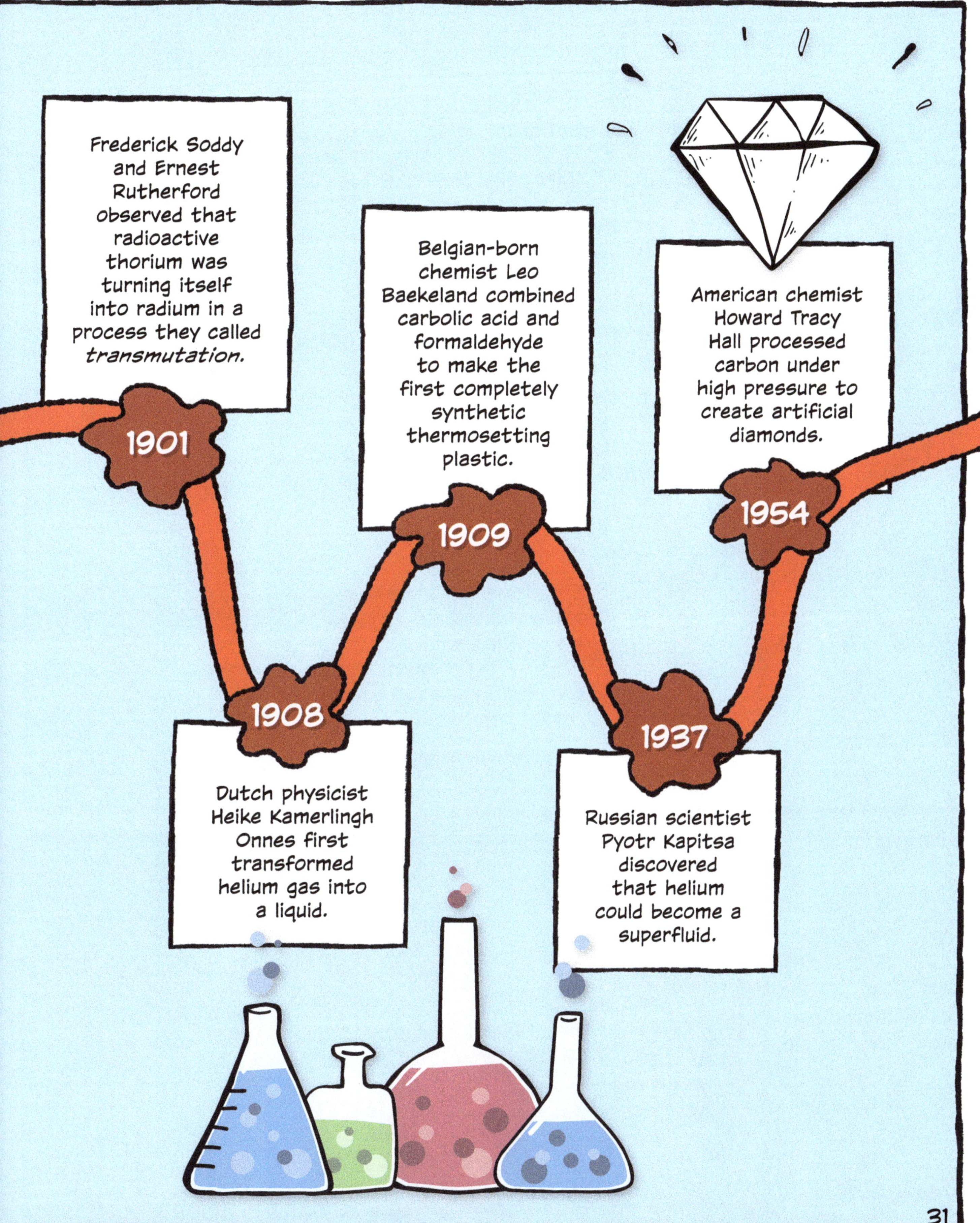
1901
Frederick Soddy and Ernest Rutherford observed that radioactive thorium was turning itself into radium in a process they called *transmutation.*
1908
Dutch physicist Heike Kamerlingh Onnes first transformed helium gas into a liquid.
1909
Belgian-born chemist Leo Baekeland combined carbolic acid and formaldehyde to make the first completely synthetic thermosetting plastic.
1937
Russian scientist Pyotr Kapitsa discovered that helium could become a superfluid.
1954
American chemist Howard Tracy Hall processed carbon under high pressure to create artificial diamonds.

WHO'S WHO: MARIE SKŁODOWSKA CURIE
All matter is made up of chemical elements. An element is a substance that cannot be broken down into something else. Gold, carbon, and oxygen are elements.
Why, this doesn't make sense at all! There must be something else!

Who are you?
I am Marie Skłodowska Curie! I've been working to extract the element uranium from a load of pitchblende. You see, uranium atoms give off tiny particles.

But, when I remove all of the uranium from this pile of pitchblende, the material left behind gives off even more particles!
Really? Here in 1898, I thought that scientists had identified all 63* elements that make up matter.
I suspect there is another unknown element in there!

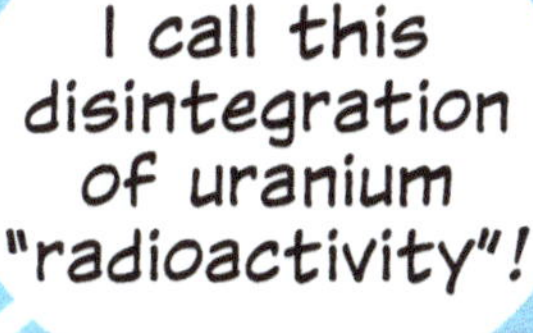

Later, scientists discovered that the polonium had formed from the uranium. Today, the process is called radioactive decay–atoms changing into other atoms!

*NOTE: In 1898, there were only 63 known chemical elements. Scientists believed they had identified all the elements that make up matter. Today, there are 118 known chemical elements.

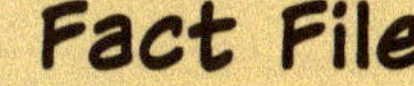

Fact File

Name: Marie Skłodowska Curie

Born: 1867 in Warsaw, Poland

Occupation: Scientist

Claim to fame: Studied radiation and how matter can undergo change that transforms one element into another.

CAN YOU BELIEVE IT?!

The metallic element mercury is naturally a liquid at room temperature. The melting temperature of gallium is so low, it will

melt in your hand!

Diamonds and graphite look very different, but both are composed of the same substance–

pure carbon.

More than

five times as much heat

is required to turn boiling water into steam as to

bring freezing water to a boil.

Electrical discharges like lightning can break up oxygen molecules in air, creating ozone. The sharp smell that you may notice after a lightning strike is

ozone.

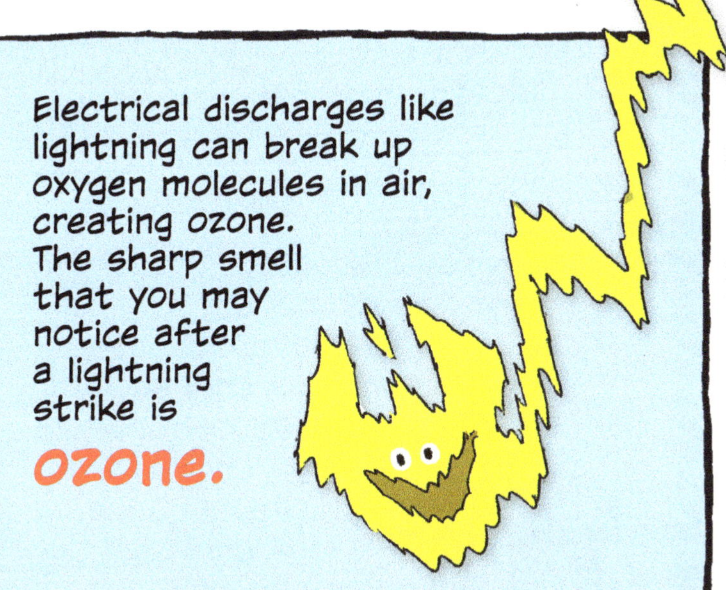
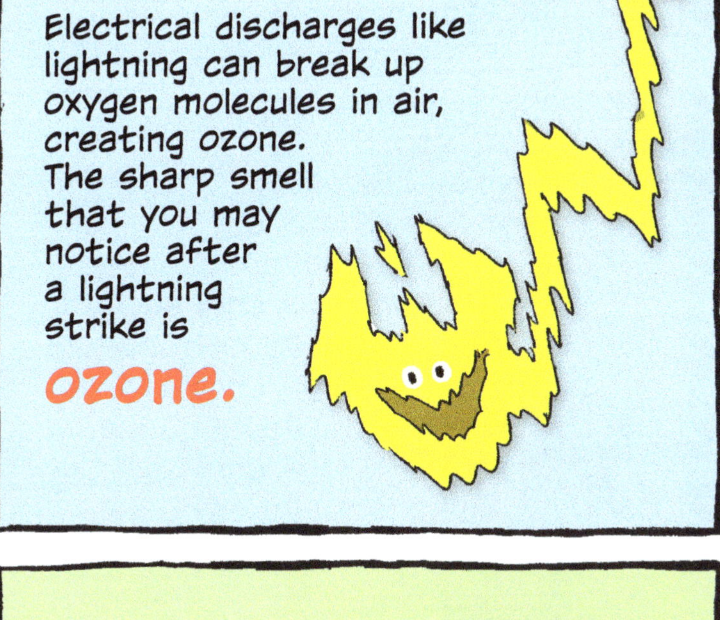

The planet Mars is called the Red Planet.

It really is red because of

iron oxide (rust)

on its surface.

Water

is a liquid at temperatures found in most places on Earth. No other common substance is liquid at ordinary temperatures.

Most substances

contract (shrink) as they grow colder. But when water is cooled, it contracts only until its temperature reaches 39 °F (4 °C). Water expands when it becomes colder than 39 °F.

For this reason, frozen water (ice) floats. If ice did not float on liquid water, life on Earth

would be impossible.

ACTIVITY: TWO WAYS TO CHANGE!

A melting ice sculpture ... a spectacular bonfire ... a cake baking in the oven ... a milkshake in the making ... an explosion: All of these involve changes in matter. Some are physical changes (changes in shape or state) and others are chemical changes (changes involving chemical reactions).

Which are which? On a separate piece of paper, for each change described below, write P for physical change or C for chemical change.

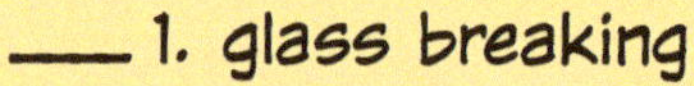

___ 1. glass breaking

___ 2. hammering wood together to build a playhouse

___ 3. a rusting bicycle

___ 4. melting butter for popcorn

___ 5. glassblower creating sculptures out of glass

___ 6. freezing chocolate-covered bananas

___ 7. separating sand from gravel

___ 8. spoiling food

___ 9. burning toast
___ 10. making salt water to gargle for a sore throat
___ 11. mixing lemonade powder into water
___ 12. cream being whipped
___ 13. water evaporating from a pond

___ 14. cutting grass
___ 15. burning leaves
___ 16. humidifier putting moisture into the air
___ 17. corroding metal
___ 18. bleaching your hair

___ 19. fireworks exploding
___ 20. squeezing oranges to get orange juice
___ 21. frying an egg
___ 22. pouring milk on your oatmeal

See page 38 for answers.

ANSWER KEY

1. P
2. P
3. C
4. P
5. P
6. P
7. P
8. C
9. C
10. P
11. P
12. P
13. P
14. P
15. C
16. P
17. C
18. C
19. C
20. P
21. C
22. P

WORDS TO KNOW

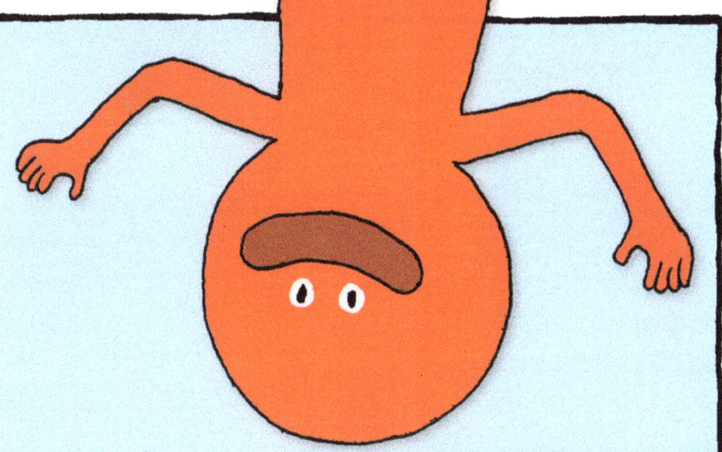

absorb to take in and hold rather than reflect.

atom one of the basic units of matter.

chemical change a change in which one substance is converted into one or more substances with different properties.

condensation the changing of a gas or a vapor into a liquid.

element a substance made of only one kind of atom.

evaporate to change from a liquid into a gas.

matter what all things are made of.

microbe a living organism of very small size.

molecule two or more atoms chemically bonded together.

nutrient a nourishing substance, especially as an element or ingredient of food.

physical change a change in which matter changes shape or form.

property a quality or characteristic of something.

solution a mixture in which one substance is dissolved (mixed completely) in another.

states of matter the different forms of matter. The most familiar are solid, liquid, and gas.

suspension a heterogeneous (uneven) mixture of a liquid and a solid in which the solid settles to the bottom if left undisturbed.

water vapor water in the state of a gas.

INDEX

www.ingramcontent.com/pod-product-compliance
Lightning Source LLC
LaVergne TN
LVHW060633110826
845147LV00014B/903
9780716650614